I0437031

The Story of a Special Day
Volume 65

March 5

64th day of the year
(65th in leap years)
301 days remaining
until the end of the year.

by Michael Dobson

Timespinner
Press

For more information about the series, about me, or
about your special day, please email us at
editor@timespinnerpress.com.

Look for other volumes in *The Story of a Special Day,*
coming often.

Table of Contents

Cover: Elvis Presley, discharged from the US Army on March 5, 1960

March 5 Quotations

"I've always wanted to make the world a more rational place. I'm still working on it."
— *Penn Jillette, born March 5, 1955*

"The people who cast the votes decide nothing. The people who count the votes decide everything."
— *Joseph Stalin, died March 5, 1953*

"I don't wanna get rich — just live good."
— *Patsy Cline, died March 5, 1963*

"A shadow has fallen upon the scenes so lately lighted by the Allied victory.... From Stettin in the Baltic to Trieste in the Adriatic an iron curtain has descended across the Continent."
— *Winston Churchill, speaking in Fulton, Missouri on March 5, 1946*

"Ignorance is an evil weed, which dictators may cultivate among their dupes, but which no democracy can afford among its citizens."
— *William Beveridge, born March 5, 1879*

Event of the Day

The Boston Massacre

Roughly five years before the start of the American Revolutionary War, tensions were already running high in the city of Boston over the unpopular Townshend Acts, which imposed tariffs on items imported from Britain. After the Massachusetts House of Representatives called for a boycott of importers, the British sent the fifty-gun warship HMS *Romney*, followed by four British Army regiments.

Riots and other clashes between civilians and soldiers became common. On February 22, 1770, a rock-throwing mob surrounded the house of a customs service employee named Ebenezer Richardson, breaking his windows. After a rock hit Richardson's wife, he fired a gun into the crowd, killing Christopher Seider, "a young lad about eleven Years of Age."

This only inflamed tensions between colonists and soldiers further. On the evening of March 5, 1770, a wigmaker's apprentice named Edward Garrick began shouting at a British officer that he had failed to pay a bill he owed. The officer, who had in fact paid the bill, ignored the complaint, but a guard, British Private Hugh White, tried to intervene. In the ensuing argument, White hit Garrick in the head with his musket, and a crowd began to gather outside the customs house where the incident took place, throwing objects at Private White and daring him to fire his weapon.

Seven British soldiers joined White, facing a crowd that had grown to over 300 people. The standoff began to escalate, until one of the colonists knocked down one of the privates, named Hugh Montgomery.

Enraged, Montgomery picked up his weapon, shouted "Damn you, fire!" and began shooting into the crowd. As the crowd surged forward, the other soldiers began to fire. Eleven men were hit, three of whom died immediately: Samuel Gray, James Caldwell, and most famously, a runaway slave named Crispus Attucks.

The riot spread to nearby streets, and the British 29th Regiment took up defensive positions. Acting Governor Thomas Hutchinson, speaking from the balcony of the state house, managed to restore partial order by promising a fair inquiry into the shootings.

The soldiers involved in the shooting were arrested, but the trials were delayed for months as a propaganda war raged. A Boston artist named Henry Pelham illustrated the event, which was turned into an engraving by silversmith Paul Revere.

The British asked lawyer and future US president John Adams to defend the soldiers. Six were acquitted, and two were found guilty of manslaughter. But the damage had been done. The Boston Massacre is credited with turning colonial sentiment firmly against the British king, George III, and Parliament, and is a key moment in the course of events that led to the American Revolution.

Illustration by Henry Pelham, engraved by Paul Revere

March 5 Holidays and Celebrations

St. Piran's Day (Cornwall, Great Britain)

Saint Piran, who is said to have come to Cornwall from Ireland, is the patron saint of tin miners and one of the patron saints of Cornwall. March 5 was originally a holiday for tin miners, but has grown to become the national day of Cornwall.

St. Piran's Flag, the flag of Cornwall

Custom Chief's Day (Vanuatu)

The island nation of Vanuatu, located in the South Pacific Ocean, consists of many islands that still live according to their traditional customs and folkways. Small villages are often ruled by chiefs in the traditional manner. On March 5, these tribal chiefs are honored in a public holiday that features sports, carnivals, agricultural fairs, and arts festivals.

Learn from Lei Feng Day (学雷锋日 (China)

On March 5, the Communist Party of China celebrates "Learn from Lei Feng Day," (学雷锋日, or Xué Léi Fēng Rì). Lei Feng, a soldier of the People's Liberation Army, is held up as a model citizen, an icon of selflessness, modesty, and devotion to Mao Zedong. Lei Feng is a cultural icon in China, and his day is celebrated with various community and school events, along with public service activities.

Christian Feast Days

Saints commemorated on March 5 include John Joseph of the Cross, Ciarán of Saigir (Irish calendar), Theophilus Bishop of Caesarea, and Thietmar of Minden.

Chinese propaganda poster for "Learn
from Lei Feng Day" by Qiu Wei (丘玮)

10

What Happened on March 5?

1836 CE – **Samuel Colt's Revolver**

After many years of work, inventor Samuel Colt designed and patented a new type of pistol that used a rotating cylinder, able to be built on an assembly line using interchangeable parts. On March 5, 1836, he founded the Patent Arms Manufacturing Company to build his first revolver, the Colt Paterson. Although this company would fail, Colt's subsequent revolvers would become legendary.

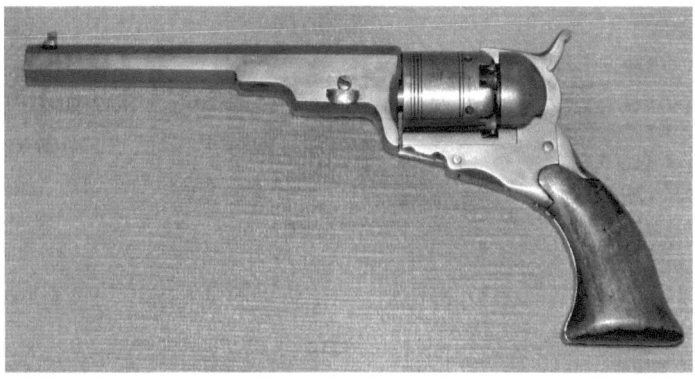

1836 CE – **Westinghouse Patents the Air Brake**

Inventor George Westinghouse witnessed a train wreck in which the two engineers saw each other, but couldn't stop their trains in time. Stopping a massive train was extremely difficult, and derailments and collisions were all too common. Westinghouse solved the problem by creating a braking system that used compressed air, which gained almost universal acceptance and in various forms is still used today.

1931 CE – **Gandhi-Irwin Pact**

The civil disobedience (*satyagraha*) movement started by Mahatma Gandhi led to a series of meetings between the Viceroy of India, Lord Irwin, and Gandhi himself. Gandhi obtained the right of the Indian National Congress to participate more fully in negotiating constitutional reforms, release of political prisoners, and removal of the highly symbolic and oppresive tax on salt. While the Gandhi-Irwin Pact fell far short of the goal of Indian independence, it was an important step nonetheless.

1933 CE – **The Nazis Take Power**
In the German federal elections of March 5, 1933, Adolf Hitler's Nazi party won 43.9% of the vote, making them the largest party in the Reichstag. Although the Nazis fell short of a majority, Hitler became chancellor in a coalition government, and managed to pass the Enabling Act, which established Hitler's power to pass laws without the Reichstag's approval, effectively making him dictator.

1940 CE – **Katyn Massacre Approved**
On March 5, 1940, Soviet secret police chief Lavrentiy Beria received approval from Communist Party general secretary Joseph Stalin to carry out liquidations of Polish nationals. At least 21,000 Poles were murdered. The Nazi government announced they had found mass graves in the Katyn Forest in 1943, but the Soviets denied involvement until their official acknowledgement of the murders in 1990.

1946 CE – **Churchill's "Iron Curtain" Speech**
Speaking at Westminster College in Fulton, Missouri, on March 5, 1946, Sir Winston Churchill, then Leader of the Opposition in the British Parliament, first used the term "iron curtain" to describe the countries of the Soviet sphere in Eastern Europe.

Winston Churchill (left) and President Harry Truman en route to Fulton, Missouri for the "Iron Curtain" speech

1960 CE – *Cover Event:* Elvis Gets Out of the Army

On March 5, 1960, Elvis Presley, who had been drafted two years earlier, received his honorable discharge from the United States Army, along with a mustering-out check for $109.54. During his 18-month stint in Germany, he met 14 year old Priscilla Beaulieu, whom he would marry seven years later.

1970 CE – **Non-Proliferation Treaty Takes Effect**

The Nuclear Non-Proliferation Treaty (NPT), which attempts to prevent the spread of nuclear weapons, was initially proposed in 1958 and opened for signature in 1968. Finland was the first nation to sign the treaty, with 43 nations needed before the treaty could take effect. On March 5, 1970, the NPT went into effect. Today, 189 nations have signed the treaty — more than have signed any other arms limitation agreement.

1975 CE – **Homebrew Computer Club**

The computer hobbyist group known as the Homebrew Computer Club, located in Silicon Valley, held its first meeting on March 5, 1975. Numerous important figures in the computer field came from its ranks, including the founders of Microsoft and Apple.

1982 CE – **Venera 14 Lands on Venus**

On March 5, 1982, the Soviet unmanned spacecraft Venera 14 (Венера-14) entered the Venusian atmosphere, landing on the surface of the planet. It survived 57 minutes in the harsh Venusian environment, sending back photographs and various scientific readings.

Computer enhanced global view of the surface of Venus, based on color images recorded by the Soviet Venera 13 and 14 spacecraft. Normally, the surface of Venus cannot be seen because it is completely shrouded in clouds.

Who Was Born on March 5?

> *The abbreviation "O.S." on some dates refers to the fact that the Russian Empire did not switch from the Julian to the Gregorian calendar at the same time as the rest of Europe, and therefore some figures have two dates for their birth or death.*
>
> *People whose original names are not in the Western alphabet have their native names in the appropriate script shown in parenthesis.*

Acting

Jake Lloyd (March 5, 1989 —)
Child actor Jake Lloyd played the young Anakin Skywalker in *Star Wars Episode I: The Phantom Menace.*

Kimberly McCullough (March 5, 1978 —)
Actress Kimberly McCullough originated the role of Robin Scorpio on the long-running soap

opera *General Hospital* in 1985 at the age of seven, and continued (with interruptions) until 2012.

Jolene Blalock (March 5, 1975 —)
Actress Jolene Blalock played the Vulcan T'Pol in the television series *Star Trek: Enterprise.*

Eva Mendes (March 5, 1974 —)
Eva Mendes is an actress, singer, and spokesmodel who has starred in a number of movies.

Marsha Warfield (March 5, 1954 —)
Comedienne Marsha Warfield is best known for playing Roz in the NBC sitcom *Night Court.*

Michael Warren (March 5, 1946 —)
Former All-American UCLA basketball star Michael Warren also played Officer Bobby Hill on the television series *Hill Street Blues.*

Samantha Eggar (March 5, 1939 —)
British actress Samantha Eggar was nominated for an Academy Award and won a Golden Globe Award for her role in *The Collector.*

Dean Stockwell (March 5, 1936 —)

Beginning as a child actor, Dean Stockwell's acting career has spanned over 65 years and nearly 100 films.

James B. Sikking (March 5, 1934—)

James B. Sikking played leading roles in the television series *Hill Street Blues* and *Doogie Howser, MD.*

Rex Harrison (March 5, 1908 — June 2, 1990)

English stage and screen actor Rex Harrison is remembered for his role as Professor Henry Higgins in *My Fair Lady,* among many other roles.

Rex Harrison (left) as Julius Caesar, with Elizabeth Taylor in the movie *Cleopatra.*

Illustration by Howard Pyle from
Howard Pyle's Book of Pirates (1921)

Art

Howard Pyle (March 5, 1853 — November 9, 1911)

Author and illustrator Howard Pyle is famous for his books for young people, including Robin Hood and King Arthur. He created what has become the modern image of pirate dress.

Business

Laurence Tisch (March 5, 1923 — November 15, 2003)

Investor and billionare businessman Larry Tisch was CEO of the CBS television network from 1986 to 1995 and co-chaired Loews Theaters.

James Tobin (March 5, 1918 — March 11, 2002)

Economist James Tobin served as a member of the Council of Economic Advisors and the Board of Governors of the Federal Reserve. He received the Nobel Prize in Economics in 1981

Momofuku Ando (安藤 百福) (March 5, 1918 — March 11, 2002)

Momofuku Ando, founder of Nissin Food Products, invented instant cup noodles.

Nissin Cup Noodles

Chess

Siegbert Tarrasch (March 5, 1862 — February 17, 1934)

Grandmaster Siegbert Tarrasch was one of the strongest chess players of the late 19th century, as well as an influential chess teacher. The Tarrasch Defense is named for him, as are Tarrasch Variations of the French Defense and the Ruy Lopez.

Magic

Penn Jillette (March 5, 1955 —)

Illusionist, comedian, and author Penn Jillette is best known for being part of Penn & Teller.

Music

Charlie and Craig Reed (March 5, 1962 —)

Scottish twins Charlie and Craig Reed formed the band The Proclaimers, best known for their hit song "I'm Gonna Be (500 Miles)."

Andy Gibb (March 5, 1958 — March 10, 1988)

Singer and teen idol Andy Gibb was the younger brother of the Bee Gees musical group (Barry, Robin, and Maurice Gibb) and had a significant solo career.

Teena Marie (March 5, 1956 — December 26, 2010)

Known as the "Ivory Queen of Soul," Teena Marie had numerous gold and platinum hits.

Politics

Canaan Banana (March 5, 1936 — November 10, 2003)

Canaan Banana was the first president of Zimbabwe, and later served as a diplomat for the Organization of African Unity.

Zhou Enlai (周恩来) (March 5, 1898 — January 8, 1976)

Zhou Enlai was the first premier of the People's Republic of China, serving from 1949 until his death in 1976.

Henry II of England (March 5, 1133 — July 6, 1189)

Henry II and his wife Eleanor of Aquitaine claimed the throne of England and controlled the Angevin empire, which covered most of western Europe. He is famous for his supposed statement "Will no one rid me of this turbulent priest?" that resulted in the murder of Thomas Becket, Archbishop of Canterbury.

Henry II of England

Religion

Joel Osteen (March 5, 1963 —)

Televangelist and megachurch pastor Joel Osteen was named one of ABC News' "Ten Most

Fascinating People" and *The Church Report's* "Most Influential Christian in America" in 2006.

Science and Mathematics

Lynn Margulis (March 5, 1938 — November 22, 2011)

Biologist Lynn Margulis is best known for her theory on the origin of eukaryotic organelles and her contributions to the endosymbiotic theory. She received the National Medal of Science in 1999 and the Darwin-Wallace Medal in 2008.

Daniel Kahneman (כהנמן דניאל) (March 5, 1934 —)

Psychologist Daniel Kahneman won the Nobel Prize in Economics for his work on the psychology of judgment and decision-making and cognitive bias.

Gerardus Mercator (March 5, 1512 — December 2, 1594)

Cartographer and mathematician Gerardus Mercator developed the Mercator projection mapping approach, still in common use today.

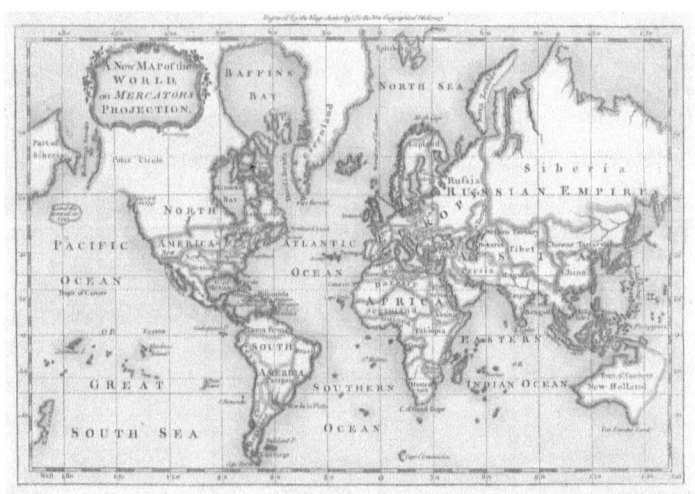

Map using Mercator projection (1766)

Sports

Tim Sylvia (March 5, 1976 —)
Mixed martial arts (MMA) fighter Tim Sylvia is a former two-time UFC Heavyweight Champion.

Michael Irvin (March 5, 1966 —)
Former Dallas Cowboy Michael Irvin was elected to the Pro Football Hall of Fame in 2007.

Fred Williamson (March 5, 1938 —)
American Football League champion Fred "The Hammer" Williamson went on to a successful career as an actor, sportscaster, and director.

Del Crandall (March 5, 1930 —)

Catcher Del Crandall played for Boston and Milwaukee. He was selected 11 times for the All-Star game, played on the winning team in the 1957 World Series, and won four Gold Glove Awards in his career.

Writing

Mike Resnick (March 5, 1942 —)

Science fiction author Mike Resnick has been nominated for a record-setting 36 Hugo Awards for writing, winning five times.

Pier Paolo Pasolini (March 5, 1922 — November 2, 1975)

Italian director, poet, writer, and intellectual Pier Paolo Pasolini is considered a major figure in Italian literature and art, and a major voice in 20th century poetry.

Who Died on March 5?

Acting

Walt Gorney (April 12, 1912 — March 5, 2004)

Actor Walt Gorney is best known for playing Crazy Ralph (who shouts "You're all doomed!") in the 1980 movie *Friday the 13th* and sequels.

Richard Kiley (March 31, 1922 — March 5, 1999)

Stage and screen actor Richard Kiley played Don Quixote in the original Broadway production of *Man of La Mancha,* and won three Emmys, two Golden Globes, and two Tony Awards.

Whit Bissell (October 25, 1909 — March 5, 1996)

Whit Bissell appeared in hundreds of films and television episodes. He is best known for roles in low-budget science fiction and horror films, for which he received a life career award from the Academy of Science Fiction, Fantasy and Horror Films. He served on the board of the Screen Actors Guild.

Gary Merrill (August 2, 1915 — March 5, 1990)

Film and television character actor Gary Merrill played numerous supporting roles in his long career. His second wife was his *All About Eve* co-star Bette Davis. He participated in the 1965 Selma to Montgomery marches.

William Powell (July 29, 1892 — March 5, 1984)

Leading man William Powell is famous for his role in the *Thin Man* films. He was nominated for three Academy Awards. His second wife was actress Carole Lombard, and he was involved with Jean Harlow up until her death in 1937.

William Powell

John Belushi (January 24, 1949 — March 5, 1982)

John Belushi was an original cast member of *Saturday Night Live.* His breakout role in 1975's *Animal House* led to other comic roles, including his partnership with Dan Ackroyd in The Blues Brothers musical act and motion picture.

Jay Silverheels (May 26, 1912 — March 5, 1980)

Native American actor Jay Silverheels played Tonto, the "faithful Indian companion" of the Lone Ranger, in the long-running TV series.

Billy De Wolfe (February 18, 1907 — March 5, 1974)

Actor Billy De Wolfe appeared as a comic actor in numerous films and television series, but is best known today as the voice of the frustrated magician in the Christmas perennial *Frosty the Snowman:* "Mess-y, mess-y, mess-y! Bus-y, bus-y, bus-y!"

Fresco by Corregio in the dome of Parma Cathedral

32

Art

Antonio da Correggio (August 1489 — March 5, 1934)

Correggio was a leading painter of the Italian Renaissance, known as the foremost painter of the Parma School.

Business

David Dunbar Buick (September 17, 1854 — March 5, 1929)

Scottish born inventor David Buick founded the eponymous Buick Motor Company in 1902. Over 35 million cars have borne his name.

Crime

Richard Kuklinski (April 11, 1935 — March 5, 2006)

Contract killer Richard "The Iceman" Kuklinski worked for the Gambino crime syndicate and other members of the American Mafia's Five Families, claiming over 100 murders. He was arrested in 1986 and died in prison.

Lena Baker (June 8, 1901 — March 5, 1945)

African-American maid Lena Baker was executed by the State of Georgia in 1945 for killing her employer, who had imprisoned her and threatened to shoot her if she tried to leave. She received a posthumous full pardon in 2005. The 2008 movie *The Lena Baker Story* is about her life.

Music

Robert B. Sherman (December 19, 1925 — March 5, 2012)

Robert Sherman and his brother Richard wrote the songs for numerous Disney films including *Mary Poppins* and *The Jungle Book,* as well as the theme park song "It's A Small World (After All)."

Yip Harburg (April 8, 1896 — March 5, 1981)

Lyricist Yip Harburg wrote such songs as "Brother, Can You Spare a Dime?" "April in

Paris," "It's Only a Paper Moon," and all of the songs for the 1939 movie *The Wizard of Oz*.

Sol Hurok (Соломон Гурков) (April 9, 1888 — March 5, 1974)

Impressario Sol Hurok managed numerous performing artists and had a huge influence on American music. He brought the Bolshoi Ballet to the United States for the first time in 1959.

Patsy Cline (September 8, 1932 — March 5, 1963)

Country music star Patsy Cline is best known for her crossover hits "Walkin' After Midnight" and "I Fall to Pieces." She is considered one of the best female vocalists of the 20th century. She died in a plane crash along with country stars Hawkshaw Hawkins and Cowboy Copas.

Sergei Prokofief (Сергéй Прокóфьев) (April 23, 1891 — March 5, 1953)

Russian composer Sergei Prokofief was one of the major clasical composers of the 20th century, perhaps best known today for *Peter and the Wolf* and the ballet *Romeo and Juliet*.

Politics

Mohammad Mosaddegh (مصدق محمد) (June 16, 1882 — March 5, 1967)

Mohammad Mosaddegh was the democratically elected prime minister of Iran from 1951 to 1953. He was overthrown in a coup d'etat with the collaboration of Britain's MI-6 and the US's CIA for nationalizing the Iranian oil industry.

Chen Cheng (陳誠) (January 4, 1897 — March 5, 1965)

Chen Cheng was a military commander in the Chinese Civil War, and subesquently served as premier of the Republic of China (Taiwan).

Joseph Stalin (Иосиф Сталин) (December 18, 1878 — March 5, 1953)

Joseph Vissaironovich Stalin was one of the original Bolshevik revolutionaries who took power in 1917. After the death of Vladimir Lenin, he consolidated supreme power in his own hands. He is notorious for the 1930's Great Purge, a period of mass repression and executions. When his alliance with Nazi Germany fell apart in 1941, he played a decisive role in the Allied victory against Germany and helped establish the satellite states of the Eastern Bloc as Soviet clients.

Joseph Stalin

Crispus Attucks (1723? — March 5, 1770)

Crispus Attucks was the first person shot to death during the Boston Massacre. Little is known of his life. He appears to have been born a slave; he was evidently of African and Native American descent. Whether he became a free man or was an escaped slave is a matter of historical debate. It is known that he became a sailor and spent much of his life at sea working on whaling ships. He became an icon of the anti-slavery movement and is considered the first martyr of the American Revolution.

Crispus Attucks

Science and Mathematics

Joseph Weizenbaum (January 8, 1923 — March 5, 2008)

Artificial intelligence pioneer Joseph Weizenbaum wrote ELIZA, a natural language processing program, and designed the Magnetic Ink Character Recognition system that allows automatic processing of checks. The Weizenbaum Award for contributions to information and computer ethics is named for him.

Alessandro Volta (February 18, 1745 — March 5, 1827)

Italian physicist Alessandro Volta invented the battery. The unit of electrical potential is named the "volt" from Volta's Law of Capacitance.

Pierre-Simon Laplace (March 23, 1749 — March 5, 1827)

Mathematician and astronomer Pierre-Simon Laplace made numerous contributions to celestial mechanics. He developed the major portion of what became known as the Baysian interpretation of probability. Laplace's equation, the Laplace transform, and the Laplacian differential operator are some of his other important contributions. He is considered one of the greatest scientists in history, and is sometimes referred to as the "Newton of France."

Franz Mesmer (May 23, 1734 — March 5, 1815)

Franz Anton Mesmer developed the theory of "animal magnetism," called "mesmerism," which led to the development of hypnotism. The word "mesmerize" comes from his name.

Sports

Pepper Martin (February 29, 1904 — March 5, 1965)

Baseball third baseman and outfielder Pepper Martin was known as the "Wild Horse of the Osage." He is best known for his role in the Cardinal's upset victory over Philadelphia in the 1931 World Series.

Writing

Herman J. Mankiewicz (November 7, 1897 — March 5, 1953)

Screenwriter Herman J. Mankiewicz co-authored 1941's *Citizen Kane* with Orson Welles, with whom he shared the Academy Award. As a credited and uncredited screenwriter, he contributed to such films as *The Wizard of Oz* and *Gentlemen Prefer Blondes.*

Edgar Lee Masters (August 23, 1868 — March 5, 1950)

Poet Edgar Lee Masters is best known for his work *Spoon River Anthology.*

The month of March, from the illuminated manuscript *Les Très Riches Heures du duc de Berry*

March: The Third Month

In ancient Rome, March was the first month of the year. As the first month of spring, in the Mediterranean climate it marked the beginning of the military campaign season. That's why March (Martius) is named in honor of Mars, the Roman god of war.

Although the first month of the year was moved back to January sometime during the transition of Rome from a kingdom to a republic (historians differ), March was the first month of the year in Russia until the end of the 15th Century, and is the first month of the year in many other cultures and religions.

In the northern hemisphere, March 1 marks the beginning of meteorological spring. In the southern hemisphere, March is the equivalent of September, making southern hemisphere March the beginning of autumn.

March is one of the seven months that have 31 days in it. March starts on the same day of the week as November every year, and except for leap years starts on the same day as February.

March starts on the same day of the week as the previous June except for leap years, and in leap years starts on the same day as the previous September and December.

March in Other Cultures

In Finland, March is called *maaliskuu* (earthy month). In Ukraine, it's *березень* (birch tree). Other names for March include *Lentmona*t (Saxon), *Hyld-monath* (Angles), and *sušec* (Slovene).

March Symbols

Birthstones: Aquamarine and bloodstone, both representing courage.

Aquamarine

Birth Flowers Daffodils

Daffodils in Bagatelle Park, Paris, France

March Events

Honorary months: Presidents, Congresses, and nations around the world issue proclamations recognizing particular months to honor certain causes. These events generally fall in March. (All US unless otherwise noted.)

- National Nutrition Month

- American Red Cross Month

- Women's History Month (celebrated in Canada during October)

- Irish-American Heritage Month

- Colorectal Cancer Awareness Month

- Fire Prevention Month (The Philippines)

Women's Suffrage picket line, 1917

"March Madness": (United States) The NCAA Men's Division I Basketball Championship, popularly known as "March Madness" or the "Big Dance," is a single-elimination tournament to establish the champion college basketball team.

Multi-day events: Some March events span multiple days.

- **Nineteen Day Fast:** (Bahá'í Faith) March 2 through March 20

Movable events: Some events change dates from year to year.

- **Mardi Gras:** French for "Fat Tuesday," this celebration takes place the day before Ash Wednesday, the beginning of the Lenten season. The New Orleans Mardi Gras celebration is perhaps the most famous, but Mardi Gras and the Carnival season (between Ephiphany and Ash Wednesday) are celebrated in many areas with large Catholic populations. Mardi Gras can take place anywhere from February 3 to March 9 in regular years, and from February 4 to March 9 in leap years.

- **Casimir Pulaski Day:** (Illinois) The first Monday in March is observed as a holiday in Illinois, in memory of the Revolutionary War cavalry officer born in Poland. Dates range from March 1 to March 7.

Mardi Gras Night Parade, New Orleans, 2012

March Zodiac Signs

From the perspective of someone on Earth, the Sun appears to move through the sky throughout the year, along a path astronomers call the ecliptic plane. The ecliptic plane is divided into twelve constellations, known as the zodiac, based on traditionally observed patterns of stars. On your birthday, you can't see your constellation, because it's part of the daytime sky.

The zodiac was first developed by Babylonian astronomers about 2,500 years ago. Because they were unaware that the Earth wobbles like a spinning top (a motion known as *precession*), they didn't make allowance for the fact that the Sun's path through the zodiac changes over time.

That means there are now two sets of dates for your birth sign. The *tropical dates* are the original Babylonian dates; the *siderial dates* tell you where the Sun actually appears as it moves along its annual path.

Zodiac signs for March 5 are Aquarius (siderial) and Pisces (tropical).

Aquarius

Tropical January 20 to February 19
Siderial February 12 to March 8 (March 9 in leap years)

Aquarius is one of the oldest recognized constellations, originally representing the Babylonian god Ea. In Latin, Aquarius means "water-carrier," represented in its symbol. In Greek mythology, Aquarius is sometimes associated with Deucalion, who survived a world-cleansing flood. In Chinese astronomy, it is known as the Black Tortoise of the North (北方玄武, Běi Fāng Xuán Wǔ).

In astrology, Aquarius is considered to be masculine and extroverted, and despite the name is an air sign. Aquarians are supposed to be philanthropical, inventive, and individualistic.

Pisces

Tropical February 20 to March 20
Siderial March 15 to April 14

In the Roman legend of Venus and her son Cupid, they escaped the clutches of Typhon, known as the "father of all monsters," by transforming into fish and tying themselves together with rope. That's why the name Pisces is plural for fish. The constellation appears as a somewhat ragged "V" shape, representing the rope, with the "fish" located at the two rope ends.

In astrology, Pisces is a water sign, compatible with the other water signs Cancer and Scorpio, as well as with the earth signs Taurus, Virgo, and Capricorn. Pisceans are supposed to be imaginative, compassionate, unworldly, secretive, and escapist.

What Day of the Week is March 5?

On what day of the week does March 5 fall?

Unfortunately, this isn't an easy question. Because the calendar year is 365 days long (366 in leap years), it doesn't divide evenly by the seven days of the week.

Also, the Earth goes around the Sun in about 365-1/4 days, so a calendar tends to drift over time. That's why the same date falls on different weekdays in different years.

This is made even more complicated by a change in calendars that took place in 1582. Our modern calendar has its roots in ancient Rome, in a calendar reform conducted by Julius Caesar. Caesar commissioned mathematicians to attack the problem, and came up with the idea of *leap years*, and thus standardized the calendar for centuries to come. This was called the *Julian calendar*.

Over time, however, the small errors in Caesar's calculation compounded. That's why Pope Gregory XIII commissioned the *Gregorian calendar*, used in most of the world today. Some countries converted in 1582, when the calendar was first developed; some converted later; other still haven't changed.

Gregorian and Julian aren't the only types of calendars. The Hebrew year, the Islamic year, and many other calendars are used in different parts of the world and among different people.

You can convert Gregorian dates to other calendars, including the Hebrew calendar, the Islamic calendar, and even the Mayan calendar by visiting the Fourmilab Calendar Converter at http://www.fourmilab.ch/documents/calendar/.

A 50-year brass perpetual calendar.

Copyright, Credit, and Contact

Follow Us

Our blog Dobson's Improbable History features short articles on events and people associated with each day, and updates several times each week. Get the latest on Twitter @SidewiseThinker.

Sources and Art Credits

All art and photographs are either in the public domain or used under a Creative Commons license. Attribution is provided where requested by the copyright owner or when of historical significance, listed below.

- The cover photograph of Elvis Presley in the US Army is believed to be an official Army photograph and thus in the public domain.

- The 1770 engraving of the Boston Massacre is in the public domain because its copyright has expired.

- The flag of Cornwall is not an object of copyright.

- The Chinese Lei Feng poster is published by the Chinese government. Its copyright status is uncertain, but this low-resolution image to illustrate the holiday is allowable under fair use provisions of the copyright law.

- The photograph of the Colt Paterson revolver is by "Hmaag" and is used under the terms of the Creative Commons Attribution-Share Alike 3.0 Unported license.

- The photograph of Winston Churchill and Harry Truman is by photographer Abbie Rowe, and is from the collection of the Harry S. Truman Library, National Archives and Records Administration. It is in the public domain.

- The photograph of Venus was created by NASA's Jet Propulsion Laboratory and is in the public domain.

- The photograph of Rex Harrison and Elizabeth Taylor in *Cleopatra* (1963) is in the public domain because the copyright was not renewed.

- The pirate illustration by Howard Pyle is in the public domain because the copyright has expired.

- The display of cup noodles was taken by Yumi Kimura and is licensed under the Creative Commons Attribution-Share Alike 2.0 Generic license.

- The illustration of Henry II of England is taken from the 1902 book *Cassell's History of England,* and is in the public domain.

- The 1766 map of the world is in the public domain.

- The screenshot of William Powell from the trailer for *The Great Ziegfield* is in the public domain because its copyright was not renewed.

- The fresco by Antonio da Correggio is in the public domain.

- The official portrait of Stalin is in the public domain.

- The engraving of Crispus Attucks is in the public domain.

- The 1933 Goudey baseball card of Pepper Martin is in the public domain because its copyright was not renewed.

- The illustration of the month of March is from the French Gothic illuminated manuscript *Les Très Riches Heures du duc de Berry* by the Limbourg Brothers, Jean Colombe, and an intermediate painter whose name is lost to history.

- The photograph of aquamarine has been released into the public domain.

- The photograph of daffodils is by Myrabella, and is licensed under the Creative Commons Attribution-Share Alike 3.0 Unported license.

- The 1917 Women's Suffrage demonstration comes from the Library of Congress, Prints and Photographs Division, LC-USZ62-31799 DLC

- The photograph of the 2012 Mardi Gras Night Parade was taken by Mills Baker, licensed under the Creative Commons Attribution 2.0 Generic License.

- The 50-year perpetual calendar photograph is in the public domain.